KU-167-369

USING THIS BOOK

Children learn to read by **reading**, *but they need help to begin with.*

When you have read the story on the left-hand pages aloud to the child, go back to the beginning of the book and look at the pictures together.

Encourage children to read the sentences under the pictures. If they don't know a word, give them a chance to 'guess' what it is from the illustrations, before telling them.

There are more suggestions for helping children to learn to read in the *Parent/Teacher* booklet.

British Library Cataloguing in Publication Data
McCullagh, Sheila K.
    Magic at midnight. — (Puddle Lane series).
    I. Title   II. Morris, Tony   III. Series
    428.6   PR6063.A165/
    ISBN 0-7214-1075-8

First edition

Published by Ladybird Books Ltd Loughborough Leicestershire UK
Ladybird Books Inc Lewiston Maine 04240 USA

Printed in England

Magic
at midnight

written by SHEILA McCULLAGH
illustrated by TONY MORRIS

This book belongs to: M I C

Ladybird Books

It was a bright moonlit night.
Tim and Tessa were on the roof
of the Magician's house when the hands
of the clock on the little tower
moved on to twelve.
The iron boy, who stood under the clock,
lifted his hammer and struck the bell.
Dong, dong, dong, dong, dong, dong,
Dong, dong, dong, dong, dong, dong.
Midnight!

"Hello!" said Tessa.
The iron boy said nothing.

"Perhaps he can't speak," said Tim.
"I don't think he's alive."

"He must be alive, if he can
strike the bell," said Tessa.

Tim and Tessa were on the roof.
The iron boy struck the bell.

Just then, the barn owl landed softly
on the roof beside them.

"Is the iron boy alive?" asked Tessa.

"He is alive in a way," said the owl.
"He was made in the magical
Country of Zorn. He can see, and
he can think. But he can't talk,
and he can't move,
except to strike the bell."

"Poor iron boy!" said Tessa. "He must
be very lonely, up here on the roof.
Could we help him to move?"

6

The barn owl landed on the roof.
"Could we help the Iron boy
to move?" asked Tessa.

"Perhaps you could," said the owl.
"The Wise Woman, who lives
in the round house in Candletown,
has a jar of magic silver water.
If someone poured the silver water
over the iron boy, he would
be able to strike thirteen on the bell.
Then he could move and talk."

"Why doesn't someone do it?" asked Tim.

"No one has thought about it before,"
said the owl.

"Could we do it?" asked Tessa.

"I expect so," said the owl.
"I'll take you to the Wise Woman
now, if you like."

"The Wise Woman has a jar
of magic silver water,"
said the owl.

He opened his wings, and Tim and
Tessa climbed onto his back.
The owl flew off, over the houses
and across the Market Square.

Tim and Tessa climbed onto
the owl's back, and
he flew off, over the houses.

He glided down to the door
of a round stone house by the river.
The windows shone in the darkness.
The owl gave a strange cry.
The door opened, and an old woman
looked out.
"I've brought two cats to see you,
Wise Woman," said the owl. "They want
some of the magic silver water,
to pour over the iron boy who stands
on the roof of the Magician's house."

The door opened, and
an old woman looked out.

"Come in," said the Wise Woman.
She opened the door wider,
and they went inside.
"Why do you want to pour the water
over the iron boy?" she asked.
"He's very useful, up there on the roof.
He strikes the hours on the bell."

"But he must be **so** lonely," said Tessa.

"He can't even walk about," said Tim.

The Wise Woman smiled. "I don't know
what the Magician will say," she said.
"But if you want to help the iron boy,
you shall."

"Come in," said the Wise Woman.
She opened the door,
and they went inside.

She picked up a little glass bottle,
and poured some silver water into it.
"If you pour three drops
of this magic silver water
over the iron boy, then
the next time he strikes midnight,
he will find that he can strike thirteen.
And when he does that,
he will be able to move and talk."

"Oh, thank you," said Tim and Tessa.
The Wise Woman put the little bottle
round Tessa's neck.

"Pour three drops of silver water
over the iron boy,"
said the Wise Woman.

The two little cats climbed onto
the owl's back, and the barn owl
flew back over the roofs of the houses
to the Magician's garden.
"You mustn't go climbing about
with that bottle," he said.
"You'll break it. I'll come back
for you tonight, at eleven o'clock."

He flew away over the trees.

Pegs shook her head when they told her
what they were going to do.
"I hope the Magician won't mind," she said.

"I'm sure he won't," said Tessa.

18

The barn owl flew back
to the garden.
''I will come back for you
at eleven o'clock,'' he said.

The barn owl was late.

The iron boy struck the bell eleven times,
and still the owl didn't come.

"What can have happened?" asked Tessa.

"I expect he's hunting," said Tim.

Another half-hour went by.

"Let's go," said Tessa. "We've got
to be there before midnight."

At that moment the owl flew down
over the trees.

A beautiful white swan was with him.

"I'm sorry I'm late," cried the owl
as he glided down. "But I met this swan.
She needs your help."

Tim and Tessa hadn't seen a swan before.

They felt a little nervous, but the swan
looked very beautiful in the moonlight.

The owl flew down over the trees.
A swan was with him.

"The owl told me that
you have magic silver water," she said.

"Yes," said Tessa. "It's for the iron boy."

"Two of my children were turned into stone
by the King of the Fire Dragons,
in the Country of Zorn," said the swan.
"They stand on the stone gate posts
in the Magician's garden.
The magic silver water is very powerful.
It might help them to become swans again.
Will you pour some over their heads
and see?"

"Will you pour magic silver
water over the stone swans?"
asked the swan.

"But we need the silver water
for the iron boy," said Tim.

"You only need three drops,"
said the owl. "Three drops are enough."

Tessa thought for a moment.
"All right," she said. "But we'll have
to be quick. It's nearly midnight.
Let's go up on the roof
to the iron boy first."
The owl spread his wings, and
the cats climbed onto his back.

"Let's go up on the roof
to the iron boy," said Tessa.
The cats climbed
onto the owl's back.

The owl flew up to the clock tower.
The swan flew with them, and
alighted on the roof.
Tim and Tessa scrambled off
the owl's back, and looked down.
The iron boy was just below them.

The owl flew up to the roof.
The swan flew with them.

Tessa took the bottle, and pulled off the cap. Very carefully, she dropped three drops of the magic silver water onto the iron boy's head.

The drops splashed down. They sparkled for a moment in the moonlight.

Then they were gone.

Tessa poured three drops
of magic silver water
onto the iron boy's head.

"Is that all we have to do?"
asked Tessa.
"That's all," said the owl.
"Nothing will happen before midnight.
Quick! We must fly to the stone swans."
Tim and Tessa climbed on the owl's back.
The owl glided down to the gate posts.
Tessa poured three drops of magic water
onto the first swan.

Tessa poured three drops
of magic silver water
onto the stone swan.

The hands of the clock on the roof
of the Magician's house moved on to twelve.
The iron boy lifted his hammer,
and began to strike twelve.
Dong, dong, dong, dong, dong, dong –
"Quick!" cried the swan. "Tessa, be quick!"

The iron boy began
to strike the bell.

The owl spread his wings.
Tessa scrambled onto his back.
Dong, dong, dong –
The bell was still ringing.
There wasn't time for Tessa
to climb down. As the owl glided
over the second stone swan,
she leaned out, and poured the rest
of the magic silver water over him.
Dong, dong, dong.
Midnight!

Tessa poured all the rest
of the magic silver water
over the stone swan.

Tessa and the owl landed on the wall.
For a moment, there was silence.
And then they heard the iron boy
strike the bell once more —
DONG!

The iron boy struck the bell again —
DONG!

The moonlight shone down on the swans.
As Tim and Tessa watched,
the birds turned silvery white.
The hard stone softened into feathers.
The swans lifted their wings.
There was a wild cry from
the swan on the wall, and
the three birds flew up into the sky.
They circled over the Magician's garden,
and then flew off westwards,
over the trees.

The swans lifted their wings,
and flew up into the sky.

The cats watched them until
they were out of sight.
"They've gone," said Tessa rather sadly.

"They'll come back," said the owl.
"But they won't stand on the gate posts.
They'll swim on the lake. They're free now.
They'll come flying back."

"What has happened to the iron boy?"
asked Tim.

"Let's go and see," said the owl.

"Let's go and see the iron boy,"
said the owl.

As they flew up over the roof,
Tessa cried out, "There's no one there!"
The place where the iron boy had stood
was empty!
The owl swung closer over the roof.
There was no sign of the iron boy.
"The iron boy must be alive,"
said the owl. "He's gone."

The owl glided down to the garden,
and Tim and Tessa got off his back.
"I'm glad he's gone," said Tim.
"He'll be much happier, now he's alive."

"I'm glad, too," said Tessa. "But
I hope they'll all come back, one day."

They flew over the roof.
The iron boy had gone.

Notes for the parent/teacher

Turn back to the beginning, and print the child's name in the space on the title page, using ordinary, not capital letters.

Now go through the book again. Look at each picture and talk about it. Point to the caption below, and read it aloud yourself.

Run your finger along under the words as you read, so that the child learns that reading goes from left to right.

Encourage the child to read the words under the illustrations. Don't rush in with the word before he/she has had time to think, but don't leave him/her struggling.

Read this story as often as the child likes hearing it. The more opportunities he/she has of looking at the illustrations and **reading** the captions with you, the more he/she will come to recognise the words.

If you have several books, let the child choose which story he/she would like.

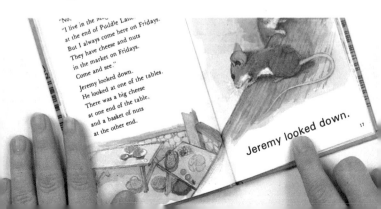

"No, I live in the mill at the end of Puddle Lane. But I always come here on Fridays. They have cheese and nuts in the market on Fridays. Come and see."

Jeremy looked down. He looked at one of the tables. There was a big cheese at one end of the table, and a basket of nuts at the other end.

Jeremy looked down.

17